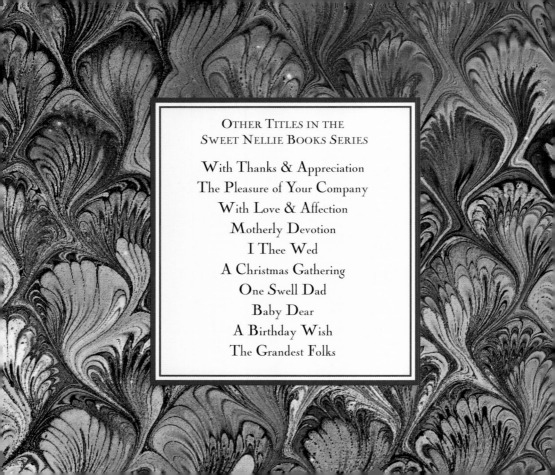

OTHER TITLES IN THE
SWEET NELLIE BOOKS SERIES

With Thanks & Appreciation

The Pleasure of Your Company

With Love & Affection

Motherly Devotion

I Thee Wed

A Christmas Gathering

One Swell Dad

Baby Dear

A Birthday Wish

The Grandest Folks

SON IN
A MILLION

To ————————————————————

From ————————————————————

Son, thou art ever with me, and all that I have is thine.

—Luke 15:31

SON IN A MILLION

The Sweet Nellie Book of
Traditional Sentiments, Endearments,
& Appreciations from the Past

PAT ROSS

VIKING
STUDIO
BOOKS

VIKING STUDIO BOOKS

Published by the Penguin Group

Penguin Books USA Inc., 375 Hudson Street, New York, New York 10014, U.S.A.

Penguin Books Ltd, 27 Wrights Lane, London W8 5TZ, England

Penguin Books Australia Ltd, Ringwood, Victoria, Australia

Penguin Books Canada Ltd, 10 Alcorn Avenue, Toronto, Ontario, Canada M4V 3B2

Penguin Books (N.Z.) Ltd, 182–190 Wairau Road, Auckland 10, New Zealand

Penguin Books Ltd, Registered Offices:
Harmondsworth, Middlesex, England

First published in 1994 by Viking Penguin,
a division of Penguin Books USA Inc.

1 3 5 7 9 10 8 6 4 2

Copyright © Pat Ross, 1994
All rights reserved

ISBN 0-670-85009-8
CIP data available

Printed in Singapore
Set in Nicholas Cochin
Designed by Virginia Norey and Amy Hill

INTRODUCTION

The definition of a fine son has altered and softened since stern Victorian parents expected little—and not-so-little—boys to set a proud example and conform to the rigid role of the era. Keeping a "stiff upper lip" was not simply an adage; it was an expectation. Yet then as now, mothers and fathers also spoke warmly of their sons as companions and friends. Their pride was infused with the same affection and regard that we feel today. That much has not changed, though much about today's relationships would cause apoplexy among the traditionalists of the past.

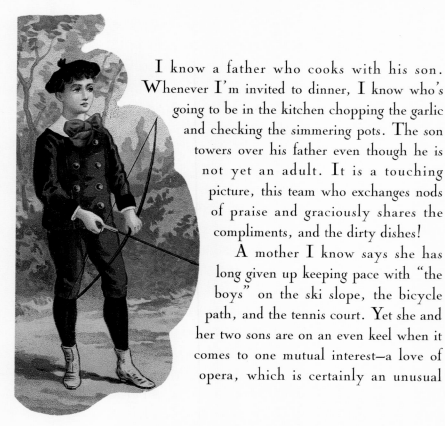

I know a father who cooks with his son. Whenever I'm invited to dinner, I know who's going to be in the kitchen chopping the garlic and checking the simmering pots. The son towers over his father even though he is not yet an adult. It is a touching picture, this team who exchanges nods of praise and graciously shares the compliments, and the dirty dishes!

A mother I know says she has long given up keeping pace with "the boys" on the ski slope, the bicycle path, and the tennis court. Yet she and her two sons are on an even keel when it comes to one mutual interest—a love of opera, which is certainly an unusual pastime for a mother and her teenage sons. When I visit for a weekend, I am always surprised to hear Puccini and Verdi mixed with rap and rock. One son has sung in the children's choir at the Metropolitan Opera. The other son needs little prompting to recite the usually tangled and melodramatic story of an opera like some stand-up comic. Their mother-son evenings at the Met may hold limited appeal for others, but it surely works for them!

Son in a Million is a thoughtful recognition of all the good times we spend with our sons, regardless of how we spend them.

A
GOOD
SON

good son is a gift of God.

—Ptahhotep
The Proverbs of Ptahhotep
c. 2400 B.C.

Every man's the son of his own deeds.

—Miguel de Cervantes Saavedra
Don Quixote
1605

Sons are the props of a house.

—Greek proverb

And all to leave, what with his toil he won,
To that unfeathered, two-legged thing—a son.

—John Dryden
Absalom and Achitophel
1682

A virtuous son is the sun of his family.

—Hindu proverb

HIS
MIRROR
IMAGE

A wise son maketh a glad father.

—Proverbs 10:1

It is not flesh and blood but the heart
which makes us fathers and sons.

—Friedrich von Schiller
Die Räuber
1781

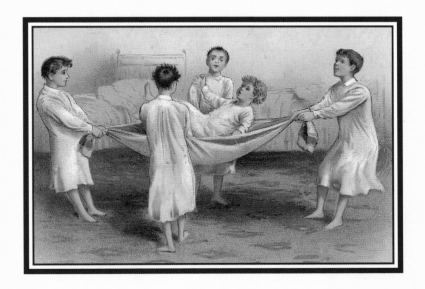

The son imbibes a portion of the intelligence, refinement, and habits of the father, and he shares in his associations.

—James Fenimore Cooper
The American Democrat
1838

There must always be a struggle between a father and a son, while one aims at power and the other at independence.

—James Boswell
The Life of Samuel Johnson
1763

LEONTINE: An only son, sir, might expect more indulgence.
CROAKER: An only father, sir, might expect more obedience.

—Oliver Goldsmith
The Good-natur'd Man
1768

He dies only half who leaves an image of himself in his sons.

—Carlo Goldoni
Pamela Nubile, II
1757

The child's the father
of the man.
—An old saying

A
MOTHER'S
HEART

Mothers, she was a mother worthy of a son.

Her anxious desire was to do justice to his better feelings, and while she wished to educate his mind, she was more anxious that his heart should be won and taught.

—T. S. Arthur
Our Homes
1866

He was tenderly attached to his mother, whose parting words seemed to enfold him like his own good genius, whose letters give him fresh strength, and warm and illumine his heart.

—Frances Bennett Callaway
*Charm and Courtesy in
Letter-Writing*
1895

I used to watch from my window in the rue Bergere in Paris. Every morning, after he had brought in the wood and swept off the doorstep, he came round, when ready for school, to the window where his mother was working, took off his cap and rose on his tiptoes to receive her kiss on his forehead. And then he saluted and marched away.

—William H. Carruth
Letters to American Boys
1907

A good man always has a bit of his mother in him, and is apt to be sympathetic and tender in his home relations because of the woman-part of his nature.

—Margaret E. Sangster
The Art of Home Making
1898

The French woman of the better class is most entirely at home and intensely agreeable, and her son is the best son in the world. He never greets her without kissing her hand; he gives her his arm for her walk; he brings her favorite arm-chair and footstool and her book; he pays her reverence and pretty compliments—he is what every son should be, but which, alas! few American sons are.

—Mrs. John Sherwood
Manners & Social Usages
1884

Why good women should be so insanely jealous on the score of their marriageable sons, as some of them are, is a neverceasing puzzle. They may not express themselves frankly as did one benignant matron who smilingly declared that she likes girls until they begin to like her sons, but they do maintain a sleepless watchdog sort of vigilance lest Jack and Max shall lose their hearts. In their views a princess is a detrimental if courted by their sons.

—Margaret E. Sangster
Good Manners for All Occasions
1904

If you mothers through weakness bring up your sons to be selfish and to think only of themselves, you will be responsible for much sadness among the women who are to be their wives in the future.

—Theodore Roosevelt

THE
DUTIFUL
SON

The whole life of a man or woman is colored by the environment and atmosphere of his or her early childhood.

—Lillian Eichler
Book of Etiquette
1922

A lifetime is not too much to spend in the investigation of the structure of the earth; but in three months an intelligent boy can learn enough of "rock and tree and flower water" to give a new interest and beauty to every landscape on which his manhood's eye may rest.

—Gail Hamilton
Country Living and Country Thinking
1862

Never allow a child to be uncourteous and disrespectful, in language or behavior, to yourself or others. Cultivate the affections with greater care than you would nurse a house plant; they afford more pleasure in the domestic circle, and their frailty demands your utmost attention.

—Mrs. L. G. Abell
The Lady's Domestic Annual
1847

A truly polite boy will not think of his own pleasure only, but will do all he can to make others happy. A selfish boy may be very polished and graceful, but he will not be a real gentleman.

—American Tract Society
My Picture-Book

The government of the family should rest upon love rather than fear. The only true obedience is that inspired by love. The child that is whipped, or coerced under fears of brutal punishment, will one day become either desperate or cowed.

—A. E. Davis
American Etiquette and Rules of Politeness
1882

If we wish our sons and daughters to possess easy, polished manners, and fair powers of expressing themselves, we should treat them politely and kindly, and lead them to take an interest in whatever conversation may be going on.

—Author unknown
Good Manners: A Manual of Etiquette in Good Society
1870

In doing away with the old and arbitrary ruling that children should be seen and not heard, we Americans have allowed our young people to run quite wild in the new liberty accorded them, and the little American girl and her brother have earned a very unsavory reputation in foreign countries, where their ready expression of quite unsolicited opinions, their forwardness in seizing a part and voice in conversations that do not concern them, and their promptitude in giving unasked advice, inspires not admiration for their undeniable intelligence and independence, but profound amazement at the lack of modesty and good breeding they display.

—Emily Holt
Encyclopedia of Etiquette
1921

CONDUCT
BECOMING

Preparation for your life-calling should not be deferred too long.

—A. E. Davis
American Etiquette and Rules of Politeness
1882

That parent who trains his child for some special occupation, who inspires him with a feeling of genuine self-respect, has contributed a useful citizen into society.

—John H. Young
Our Deportment
1882

"**A** parent who sends his son into the world without educating him in some art, science, profession or business, does great injury to mankind as well as to his son and to his own family, for he defrauds the community of a useful citizen and bequeaths to it a nuisance."

—Attributed to Chancellor Kent
American Etiquette and Rules of Politeness
1882

Self-respect is one of the necessary conditions of a true manhood. It saves one from engaging in the thousand little dishonorable things that defile the character and blast the reputation.

—A. E. Davis
American Etiquette and Rules of Politeness
1882

The Main Essentials for Good Child Manners—Respect, obedience and regard for the rights of others, the virtue which is generally known as "fair play," are three essential virtues which must be taught every child whose parents wish it to develop the proper manly or womanly qualities fostered by good manners in the true sense.

—Frederick H. Martens
The Book of Good Manners
1923

As they mature into young men and women, children repay the abundant sympathy that they have received, from their childhood up to manhood and womanhood, with abundant sympathy in return.

—Mrs. H. O. Ward
Sensible Etiquette
1878

It seems fitting that a book about traditions of the past should be decorated with period artwork. In that spirit, the art in *Son in a Million* has been taken from personal collections of original nineteenth- and early-twentieth-century drawings, advertising cards, photographs, and other paper treasures of the time.

The endpapers and chapter openings contain a pattern reproduced from a favorite vintage paper.